Shakespeare
&
Stein

Walk Into a Bar

Katherine Hastings

"not a set of rules but a harmony of whims"
Rubèn Darìo

SPUYTEN DUYVIL
New York City

ACKNOWLEDGEMENTS

Some of the poems in this collection first appeared in the following journals and anthologies: *Verde Que Te Quiero Verde: Poems after Federico García Lorca* (Natalie Peeterse, editor); *California Quarterly; Circular Philosophies; riverbabble; Spillway; Third Wednesday; Changing Harm to Harmony: Bullies & Bystanders Project* (Joseph Zaccardi, editor); *Digging Our Poetic Roots — Poems from Sonoma County*; and *Slow Shadow/White Delirium*, a collaborative chapbook with Lee Slonimsky.

Library of Congress Cataloging-in-Publication Data

Hastings, Katherine.
[Poems. Selections.]
Shakespeare & Stein walk into a bar / Katherine Hastings.
pages ; cm
ISBN 978-1-941550-79-3
I. Title.
PS3608.A86145A6 2016
811'.6--dc23
2015032095

for Cathy

CONTENTS

I   FIRST MEASURE

First Measure   5

II   SHAKESPEARE & STEIN WALK INTO A BAR

Forward to the section	9
4	11
79	12
7	13
118	14
5 (Mama Mia, Mama Thornton)	15
5 (Down the hill between the roses)	16
12	17
57	18
70	19
9	20
14	21
100	22
2	23
60	24
154	25
34	26
120	27
147	28

III FIRST MUSIC, LAST MUSIC

At Sea	33
Son	34
Portland Waltz	35
Her Troubles	36
Dear Ashraf Fayadh	37
Something About the Threat of Death	38
Give it Back	39
Drought	40
California Woodlands	42
Grazing Land	44
First Music, Last Music	46
Ten a.m.	48
Spring Lake	49
Immigration	50

IV ONCE AGAIN, THOUGHT APHRODITE

Blue and Gold	55
Menor	56
Garden Sonnet	57
On La Alameda	58
Torch	59
Light Shatters	60
The Tyrants and the Gone Daughter	61
Fossil	62
Motorcycle Diary in Progressive Mode	64
Motorcycle Rispetto	66
Còmo Se Dice	67
North Coast Dagwood	68
Autumn Drift	69
Love in the Sudden Absence of	71
Nurses	72

Gypsy Mirror   73
The Priestess Sings the Blues   74
Dark Syllable   76
Unfurling   77
Cold Moon   78

V   VISITATIONS TO THE CRYSTAL BALL

Four Mirrors
                        Hunger   83
                        Death   85
                        The Sun   86
                        October   87

Visitations to the Crystal Ball   88

VI   POSTSCRIPT

Postscript   97
What Flesh, Poetry!   99

NOTES TO THE POEMS   101
FIRST LINES OF NUMBERED SONNETS   103
ABOUT THE AUTHOR

Shakespeare & Stein
Walk Into a Bar

I
First Measure

First Measure

This morning we sail at the base
of the sky's western arm, a hut of weavers
singing full-bellied through the leaves.

Outside the cavern of trees, wind-worn
yellow grass, white deer nibbling the flow.
A woman in a suit of straw has emptied

a cup of light. Her face is a loosened knot.
The sun, slit by beech and bay, pours
fragrantly a promise of being whole.

The moon rises, is lashed to our lids.
The late breeze-brush on our bodies
asks its question: Where to go from here?

II
Shakespeare & Stein
Walk Into a Bar

Forward to the poems in this section

The poems in "Shakespeare & Stein Walk Into a Bar" use the last word of each line of the corresponding Shakespeare sonnet. This is where any similarity to the bard's poems ends. "Stein," of course, refers to Gertrude Stein. The poems that address paralysis, "14" and "100," refer to my mother, Kate Bingham, who lived the last five years of her life paralyzed. The two poems titled "5" have intentionally cut the last two lines from the Shakespeare sonnet. As far as form is concerned, these poems aren't meant to be perfect sonnets, but were allowed to create their own rhythms, as their subjects desired.

4

Shakespeare & Stein walk into a bar. They spend
in the bar a day or two or a day times four talking legacy.
Lo, lo, lo! sayeth William, pointing to his thunder. *Lend
me the stars and I will set them wherefore etc., to be free.*
Gertrude four times in four ways says *Alice Alice Alice. Abuse
not my ears,* says Shakespeare, *for my name is ungored. Give
me fourteen straight lines, two indented, like so, to use
and I wil(t) see thyself in decay. You say you live*
Gertrude in a bar sniffs on a stool with four legs. *Alone
is alone is alone, I say.* Will, over an olive: *Don't deceive
yourself, Gertie, the gracious light shines on me! Gone
are the gusts of your lifting belly and tender buttons.* They leave.

Windows reflect two bards breasting through their pain. *Thee,*
they whisper in unbarred shadows, *ye, you, thee will always be.*

79

What were my golden locks worth before love's aid
transformed them from falsely named *gentle grace*
to rolling snakes, my head crowned with hissing. Decayed
to nothing are lies of sweet subservience and hiding in this place.
On the beauty of my eyes, named *love-inspiring*, no argument.
But I prefer these whorls of blood in the whites as I pen
my history — an independent woman no god or goddess could invent
or destroy. My skin, called *roseate and milk-white* again
and again, turns green as the grass, as the woods, as the word
itself. To this woman or that man or to myself I will give
slithering hair, bleeding eyes, the pasture of my skin to afford
the freedom to walk with one, or alone, to love and live

with a curse that is not at all a curse, as those on high say,
but deliverance, a nameless liberation for which even you would pay.

7

In number seven I tell you I have willfully ripped the light
of your word and placed it on my own page, its undereye
lined with nothing remotely familiar to you. The sight
of these lines ending with your words holds no majesty.
On the contrary, they are pushed up and plunged from the hill
of emotion only an American woman of a certain age
would scribe. Vietnam, Gertrude Stein, Moms Mabley…still,
there's a filament of connection in this brazen pilgrimage.
Forgive me, Will, if I offend your pen, your eye, your ear.
These (un)sonnets are meant to be broken as light breaks into day.
Some look forward or back, some don't. Wherever you are,
feel free to throw a mistress or a jack, to look the other way.

The stars might judge one's creation. The sky may jeer at noon.
Exonerate this non-syllabic daughter, liberation for the son.

118

There are spiderlings whose motherlings are keen
to whet their appetites. For formula, real spiderwomen urge
their sacklings to dissolve them from the inside out, unseen
until the feast is finished, the selfless superhero mother-purge.
Some mothers circle their babes with silky sweetness
then tap and tremble the web to rouse their feeding
nature, a frenzied swarm of deathstrike to mother meetness.
Leggy mama awakens them and their needing,
presses herself into them, doesn't bother to anticipate
the split second between dinner-bell vibration and assured
mother-eating. Once, in an unsacrificing state
a boy-man smacked a spider with his shoe, thought it cured

his fear until her thousands of babes, poisonless but true,
sprang forth with *What has your mother done lately for you?*

5

Mama Mia, Mama Thornton, Moms Mabley, your frame
is the frame is the breath is the beat is the jazz where we dwell.
Mother Theresa, Mother Mary, Mother Jones, all the same
blues news and be-bop biscuits baked up in blackened caves. Excel
excellent Earth Mother and the nurse named Freeborn, go on
with your love of the song and the sound and the rushing water there,
there, pouring into the bowl washing the hands of Gertrude. Gone
is the gone is the gone that square mother of squarer words. Everywhere
under the earth mothers' dreams birth and mingle. Hound dogs and Picasso left
cubed bones, white robes and blue robes wipe softly hot breath from glass.

O Mother may I, may we, speak of them? We're not crying babes bereft
of longing or blue as blues singers. We're mothers every man of us, or was.

5

Down the hill between the roses, your suffering frame
bends to a patch that knows nothing of illness. *Dwell
in the new of nature's design*: a sign. Grass holds the same
message as stone. In Hawai'i the natives excel
in making *death* sound beautiful, in the air, on
the tongue. *Make, make loa, kona make.* There
the word for *her*, the one you lost, is not *gone*
but the same as the leeward wind: *kona*. Everywhere
you look you see the blue green fragrant world left
behind. You see her small face each morning in the glass.

Each day down the hill between the roses, you are bereft.
and will be, even as you see what she is, not what she was.

12

Hubba hubba mamacita the first line has to do with time.
Even if we start in the cold blue morning we'll make our way to night.
Oh night oh night oh night you were the hot red wheel of our prime
when we'd stroll from bar to bar band to band on the clean white
walks of loneliness. Skirts and shirts waved to the beat like leaves
on a trembling tree and it was easy then to go along with the herd.
We talked astrology and Earth shoes and scribbled sheaves
of phone numbers on matchbooks. We were free as the beard
of Walt Whitman, as cool as Keystone Corner, ready to make
out make up make do make a scene make every off work moment a go.
Whose lips were waiting, whose tongue? Who could forsake
the explosion of the butterfly the rainbow bus the scent of the grow?

Under the bridge the carrier carried white-capped men of defense.
In the holds they held themselves and will rock themselves hence.

57

Heat and radiance, a hot river of gems, tend
to speak directly from your body to my desire.
No other splendor but your form could spend
me in this candled light or in time require
a thought quick or deep in regret of this hour.
No need to deceive ourselves with excuses; you
say the history of us is honeysweet with a touch of sour.
Conscienceless, we embrace and whisper *adieu*,
cradle the font, the vessel, the dream, the thought
of lovers strolling barefoot in dew, and I suppose
a weed or two, something tattered and wild. Naught
threat, naught rip of the roots, just a planting of those

unconflicted seeds, a quick-breath whorled will
rocking us on a sea of need and, for now, forgotten ill.

70

In the Torah the number 70 appears without defect.
70 elders of the nation, 70 languages fair,
70 nations of the world and 70 members suspect
in Jacob's family come to Egypt. 70 thrown in the air
is a double-sided coin, ultimate unity and, we know you approve,
the epitome of disunity. 70's vibration is sensitivity, a time
of mastery and contemplation. The number of spiritual love,
the energy of the mystics. 70 is masculine energy, male prime,
though it may not seem so. You *have* passed the ambush of young days
but you've passed them, the Tarot says, on a chariot. You've charged!
You are the thinker, the dreamer, the philosopher we praise
for leaving one world for another: imagination enlarged.

70: You link the known with the unknown, show
transcendence. For this, 7 is powerful, but it is 0 you owe.

9

If you look into the imaged skyscraper of her eye
what alleys would slither there, what kind of life?
Would you find Gertrude Stein's spirit didn't die
or a series of girls with kitten-like breasts, aspiring wives?
How can she say with a dream for a mouth *Don't weep*?
She never feared leaving the men with their rings behind.
Let them pick up the emptied bowl from the floor and keep
the jewels, the fractured bits of porcelain, gray-chipped mind.
If you look into the skyscraper of her eye, how will you spend
the rest of your down-home American life? Will it
be what the pilgrims frothed up bland and bitter in the end
or will you have cherries rolling 'round your mouth? Admit it:

Your mother grew up in a dirt floor room, gloveless. "Dead," she sits
in a cloud over the city reading mystery books. She commits.

14

She wanted to leave, to take a walk, to bend and pluck
pitched stars of abandoned wishes, a paved astronomy.
There was an aching in that want, for moving parts of luck
that would guide her from paralysis to quality.
She wanted her life to be her own. She wanted to tell
everything — the parking meters, garbage cans and wind —
she, too, knew home economics had nothing to do with, well,
being a human let alone a woman. She wanted to find
her green thumb again but, even more, to somehow derive
out of all of her old loves, one true love, the salty art
of sweat and hair and fingers, mangled sheets, to thrive
away from the grave of love, to take her useless body and convert

every nerve into hot fuses that would never prognosticate
but would leap from the wheels, pick up the phone, make a date.

100

The white cat is invisible weaving her long
body around the chair of wheels. One might,
if listening to her deep vibrating song,
make from the darkness an appeal for light.
But in the long night the wheels have nothing to redeem.
Memories of a red dress, a dance, a wild life spent
beneath lemon trees high in the Starlight Room. Esteem,
when paralysis arrived, walked out the door without argument
muttering *grave, grave, grave,* began its bleak survey
of hunger for legs and wind-whipped hair, leaving her there,
the woman once called sweet and sexy things to decay
along with her abandoned will, exhausted ashes everywhere.

I sit in Amen Corner, smoking and smoking the life
out of me. I hope! Goddamn it, there's beauty in a knife.

2

But let us not be all darkness and furrowed brow.
There is laughter in the memory of a flowered field.
If the only song we can sing is *now now now*
let us sing in chorus songs of love sweetly held
in our hearts' defended pockets, untroubled by lies.
There are baby deer and pelicans sharing our days
and shining white undersides of fish with plattered eyes.
The clouds! The clouds! How can we walk without praise
of the softly floating boats we dream to use,
those rose- and leaf-embedded flight carpets of the mind.
We are temporary prisoners of the world, but that's no excuse
to entomb life's shimmering thread of joy that is thine.

We will engraft budding hope to the despair of old,
chip away the crust over kindness to the opposite of cold.

60

We escape our selves by walking along the shore.
Nearby the cliffs are high and, in the end,
more skilled with the vertigo of loss than I. Before
the day drops out of sight we silently contend
with floating above language, above what we know, light
in its western fall squandered over the world newly crowned
with doubling, re-doubling stars. Side-by-side loners, we fight
off the pull to feel as the cards tell us we should. Confound
the messages of unity spoon-fed to heart-sick youth!
As we stroll, which is to say the ten of us at least, your brow
changes shape like a cloud, your arms, I speak the truth,
are tender creatures ready for the service of love. They mow

down the pain of the past where I often take a stand,
bury fear for good, again; singing life passed hand to hand.

154

When love is young it rarely falls asleep
nor does it twist in sheets of revenge or brand
surrounding air with thick green ink to keep
upon the altarpiece of doubt a heart, a hand.
The rotted apples of war are tossed to the fire
or, dropped from chill-stricken tongues, warmed
by the revelation of, the unfolding leaf of, desire.
Every blossom, every bud bloom opens disarmed
to conjugate against the wind, unencumbered by
droughts of approval or permission, perpetual,
songless, wingless crows cawing their remedy
in their circle of lonely cures — a puritanical thrall.

In the sky, sharp contrasts of blue and white prove
pure undulation of, licked and living teeth of, love

34

Ave Maria, you say to me. *Hail Mary*, every moon and day.
You light a candle, kneel to the hem of my blue cloak.
Holy Mary Mother of — then you're on your way
to treat me as virgin slut, endless giver, womb of coal and smoke.
I come from old times, more ancient than myself, break
the darkness with light of Isis, Diana, Shingmoo, face
paradises and ghettos, long for a mouth to speak
of water-fishers, oil-fishers — moneyed men of disgrace.
What you wrought upon the mother, a planet blue with grief.
What we can see of the mother's sadness from the stars. Loss
of the elephant bird is the loss of you, there is no relief.
Loss of the Ascension Night Heron and King Island Emu cross

out, ex out, every promise made. In the cup, not one tealeaf sheds
less than a million tears, or black-inks the accounts of those deeds.

120

The newspapers are calling them the Charleston 9 now
and we wonder how their families are meant to feel.
How many black lives are required for the public to bow
to a moniker. Charleston 1? 2? 7? The steel-
hearted racist who murdered the innocents has shaken
the pot that has never rested, nor could. No sense this time,
or the last or the next. Just the final word of each line taken.
In court the families of Mother Emanuel forgave the crime.
Nine victims shot multiple times and still love remembered
to forgive, hoping for transcendence. The question hits
the center: Will it ever come? A fearful country tendered
a chair, a bible study, a badge, opens fire. Now the usual fits

of flowers. As in Oakland, Baltimore, Florida, as in…. ugly fee
for memory, another death rattle day in America. *Countrymen lend me*

147

In the hills over Granada where my old friends the crickets still
tremble in ribbons, they are digging up my bones.   Disease
of history, disease of history and its bloody lens, media event, ill
eyeball of mystery, dig us *all* up, *all* the missing dreams, please.
Sweet little Lorca bones, you are no sweeter than the rest of love
lost here, the toothless smiles and sunflowers mistaken for men kept
in this terminal of death.   We all climb the ladder, ceaselessly, approve
every adornment of heartache, every infusion of màgico, except
for the roots of memory shaped like tongues crying *Fire!* Take care
with the hoe, with the sieve, lift with caution our particles of unrest.
Whisper, *Let me see you, poet. Let me see you, preciosa.* We are
gypsies forging, dancers sobbing, winds exploding, expressed

flames encircling you. Angels all, we heave our nakedness, our bright
dove-white nakedness, uncoil the vertex of mad voices in the night.

III
First Music,
Last Music

At Sea

some morning, gazing up
to the flight field of doves
released and heading to shore,

all you'll know will be clouds
and their pale reflection of you
standing among another emptiness, ˙

everything familiar plucked
by the quick talons of time.
Out your window, fog drifts

over poplars like smoke from
blown out candles. *It's the calm before...*
You know it's someone's birthday —

Whose, did you say? Memory,
a castaway adrift, anchor line cut,
careens, repeats itself on a cleared deck,

is overcome by — what is it?
A guiding star
dropped cold at your feet

Son

— for Lee Slonimsky

What calms the breathless, nameless loss
when a mother is freed from earth? What
disentangles memory from reality, bearable
from unbearable, angles of the womb suddenly
sharp as cut jewels? Whose palms will press together
having never met before? Is it human nature,
even in September, to wish for the hush of snow,
to walk lonely paths in search of a white intaglio
to lie curled in as a babe, wailing *Where* to the woman?

The hand that held your head is now at rest,
but not the love that flows from breast to breast.
True comfort weighs as much as a feather —
it's time that gives strength, and though grief
never leaves, it changes. The infinities of
loss and healing offer each their length.

PORTLAND WALTZ

On a corner, out of nowhere, in matching
flower print blouse and skirt, spectacles
magnifying her right eye, the left stitched
permanently shut as if to wink *all of this*

is some cruel joke, a woman old enough
to be your grandmother, churchy leather
bag gaping open, looped over one arm,
palm floating through air towards me,

which is to say towards you, *can you spare?*
is a garden of bones. Indignity drips
from her mouth: *I don't like having to do this*,
stops breath and ability to put one foot

in front of *can you spare?* the other
to escape backwards over just one bridge
of so many. There is nowhere to go
but here on a corner with the unblessed,

supplementing Social Security, our shadows
merged on hard pavement. Tucking my bill
in her bag she asks, as if leaning against
a white picket fence between rose-studded yards,

How are things with you? Compliments
the aqua of my shirt.

HER TROUBLES

For a living she dressed the naked dead,
painted tattered lips with *Spring's First Rose*.
Sometimes a woman would raise her head

remembering the children hadn't been fed,
knowing what everyone else knows:
for a living she dressed the naked dead.

Now retired, she rises slow from her bed.
Early mornings Irish Whiskey flows.
Sometimes a woman would raise her head.

Hours at the mirror, blush and lashes spread,
glass in hand, her pasty make-up shows
for a living she dressed the naked dead.

Glass empty, face ready, husband in bed,
she drives to the store in her nighty, torn hose.
Sometimes a woman would raise her head.

She pushes her cart past the milk, past the bread,
lines it with bottles, for looks two tomatoes.
For a living she dressed the naked dead.
Sometimes a woman would raise her head.

Dear Ashraf Fayadh,

Outside my window men speak
in a tongue I do not completely
understand. These are the men
who work the soil, the vineyards,
who pray to another god and the
god's mother, who sing *you are
never alone.* We are all orphans
searching for light, harmony lost
to the stark meaning of man-made
laws. In our hearts, the poem of
Love is perfected, is the most holy
relic of Time. Dear Ashraf Fayadh,
may you live happily among the
living, neither lashed nor beheaded,
on little islands of wonder, feeling
for all the gods what they are
incapable of feeling, each word,
each brush stroke, a golden bee
bathed in the breath of heaven.

SOMETHING ABOUT THE THREAT OF DEATH

brings out the cook in me.
I hear it coming for a friend,
a pet, a poet in a foreign land

and gather gifts of bowls and spoons,
flour and eggs, ricotta and herbs.
Soon the whole house carries aromas

of spinach pies, berry tarts —
three-hundred-fifty degrees of hope.
Here is the spoon rest left behind

by my Irish mother — its shape a
small green leaf looked over by
a pink-eared bunny, his white tail

a small flag of charm on one day,
surrender on another. I beat and blend,
turn my kitchen into a laboratory

of defiance and acceptance and love.
What else do we have between now
and the end? What else would we want?

A crown of soft-peaked egg whites
on chocolate dark and bittersweet

Give it Back

I ask the night
to give back
all the sleep it has taken

but it laughs at me
as if I am a peasant
approaching the leader
of an oppressed country

I will not grovel
in the gray of dusk
I will not pray
for morning

I will wade through
the layers of dawn
as if it is murky water
leading me out of an
old dungeon

and when all the soldiers of morning
line up to arrest me
I will salute them in silence

drop to my knees
as if it is the first time
I have traveled to this
foreign land

Drought

What we didn't do
was feel small
flecks of mist

veiling from the sea.
What we didn't drink
were droplets trembled

from glistening trees.
Inhaling burned our lungs
with a desert dream —

camels walking a lake
of fish bones and feathers,
Ra nonchalantly

picking his teeth
with our ribs,
hissing *Remember*

who's god now?
On molten sheets
we whisper primal songs

unweave knotted dew,
sprinkle the wind
that stings the earth,

its arid streambed
of disconnected
puzzle pieces

making room for
what will come.
            What will come

to the ruins
of water, silent
beneath the need

of knob cone pines,
white skeletons of snow,
the whole earth tipping

            where?

California Woodlands

Darkness flat on the ground
rejects the prelude of morning.

Inside this cathedral of trees
no one is anxious for light —

not the smoke of sorrow rising
from blackened chimneys, not

the edge of night still suggesting
its mysterious powers.

Even the young bellflower
straightens its stem slowly

as if in a dream sculpted
from silence,

and the echo
of silence.

We know the fire will come,
that birds will sing to it

at first
as it colors our skin,

as it lights small candles
in our hair,

in our eyes.
Soon enough

it will come
to this fragile magic,

a titanic opening
to a world nowhere

— nowhere —
but here

GRAZING LAND

Cattle-ranching requires excessive amounts of water —
beef cattle use 12 gallons per day per cow, and dairy
cattle use 35 gallons per day per cow
      — Center for Biological Diversity (April 16, 2015)

It's an early spring morning
and I'm waiting for no one
The clock, accustomed to nipping at my heels,
lags behind feeling useless

We see you there, say the trails
leading to the forest of birds,
whispers the blank paper waiting
for the first drops of blood

I should feel embarrassed
in front of my dogs, in front of my shoes
lined up with eager tongues,
but the newspaper sits with

two-hundred-fifty dead native elk
fenced in for the preservation
of cows. There was nothing they could do
as they watched their wild kin wander off,

eat and drink freely,
or as they watched the cows graze
their subsidized acres. So they perished
of hunger and thirst on the altars

of milk and meat. Now the ranchers
want the remaining wild elk fenced in

or shot dead. Some things I would rather
not know. Just a break, a subterranean day

where there is no need to think of the sun
or the world we've left to ourselves,

its door of creation
creaking shut

First Music, Last Music

In Chocolate Canyon the Indians called me
Vileriana, *Milyan*, Indian daughter of the Chief
of the Kumeyaay — or Dieguéños, the name
given by white men after the nearest

Catholic mission. Here are vanishing words for you:
Ha, hallai. Water, moon. One day in 1882 rough
horsemen scared me from the valley floor up the mountain,
my babe heavy in my womb.   My husband,

Arthur from Boston, had gone away for coal.
I would rather be with rattlers than with those men.
I was a woman, a *sinya*, alone.
I can't tell you about the weather that day,

how many coyotes yipped in the moonlight.
I can tell you the name for sun is *Enya*, that my son
was born up on that mountain. When Enya came
an old Indian woman called *De Santas* found us.

She was the meaning of her name.
When my husband returned, he called the baby *Joseph*.
It was January 8, 1882. There were a few thousand of us,
and then hundreds, and then…

Cheyu, Kumeyaay, cheyu. Sing, tribe, sing
what's left of Vileriana, Milyan, you.

Joseph Head, American Indian. Literally born under a rock,
my uncle's father bicycled to 99, lived to 102

TEN A.M.

Warm air rises from the valley.
Deer sleep inside the redwood shade.
East of trees bearing heavy branches
strong sunlight enters the glass. The meadow
is calm and waving. We watch juncos
kick through seed, robins drink the bath.
All morning nature breathes through
leaves and needles. Her rhythm washes
all worries away. The song of the coming day
brushes the belly between mountain and sky,
accompanies the cadence of work.

What is work? Swallows nesting. Mist
turning to rain. Glaciers contracting. A woman
singing alone on a speck of mountain
beneath a cobbled heaven. *Youth comes
only once.*

Spring Lake

The lake walk begins here
sewn into a path where
mountains and sky decided
years ago for reflection

The great white heron,
the red-shouldered black bird,
the violet hummingbirds with
spinning wings, here

in the sweet bitter-free moment
of love in all her garbs,
scented with California hot-grass
perfume in April. The world

is a purse of green tranquility
even as light falls towards the sea
and insects awaken mating calls
among burgundy madrone, bats

dipping into the silent surface, drowsy
fish in darkening water — all of it
weaving together under this moon,

this moment, with its concentrated
assurance of light

Immigration

Butterflies the color of fortune cookies
hang upside down one second at a time
in the purple flowered brush
beneath the sunset roses.

Beside them, amber bodies
race from bloom to bloom —
honeybees. It's October and the sun
bears down on bud and brick and paper

where pictures of war smear across
what someone thinks we must know today.
I try to stay with horrors of heightened force and borders —
the discarded bomb-dusted and the drowned —

but return again and again to gatherers
of nectar and pollen weaving amidst
one another, full of purpose, waging not
one complaint against someone else's

sticky little feet
dancing in their flower.

IV
Once Again,
Thought Aphrodite

BLUE AND GOLD

ferries are busy today
in the bay where white caps rise,
spit themselves into the wind,
rise again like feathers flung.

Those flecks spell our words,
white words against blue sky,
before falling into the illegible
roil of water. Beyond the bridge

the sinking sun splits above the sea.
Last night in moonlight, long fingers
of trees signed their language
the way deaf women sign.

I read one word, you another, an unfolding
of desire all the way to its center.
Look! A sea lion raises his head, watches
with liquid eyes as the bay settles, at last,

into green, the sky molten — words and water
enmeshed in the coming dark. We, too, dissolve,
two older, easy-going birds, whirring our wings,
whispering *forever* to October shadows.

MENOR

Look, they are lying in ambush for us still!
from "The Beloved Sleeps on the Poet's Breast"
— Federìco Garcia Lorca

After seventy years, Garcìa Lorca, the stars
have brought us the name of your last love.

The dusk of nightingales, the soft-necked dove,
his name, your trembling flesh, all in a box

sheltered from eyes that would eat you whole.
Juan, you whispered, *Juan*, here is my breast,

a broken moon, the dahlia of my blood.
Garcìa Lorca, but for this boy, the underground

cell of your center, you may have left Spain,
may not have been executed with the bullfighters

and one-legged schoolteacher. The more we know,
the more the clouds fill our mouths. Poeta, poeta.

In the box, an orange blossom from Granada,
a testament of desperate desire. *I can't even look*

at him!, you say. Do we wish you hadn't? No.
We cradle the coffin of poems and letters. ¡Ay

voz secreta del amor oscuro! We resume looking
for your bones, the hard ivory of your head.

We cannot break our mourning for the lily
lost before the bloom. ¿Poeta dulce, dónde están?

Where are you?

GARDEN SONNET

The tree of burgundy roses knows
beneath the shadows of thickening leaves,
ash,
bone.

In your deepest sleep you feed and you feed.
Petals bury you again.
Root into root, rot into rot —
the need to go on.

Bud to bloom, muscle to mound,
back again and back. Roses and thorns
won't reveal

which petals your eyes, which petals your arms.
When the flowers are kissed
do you feel them?

On La Alameda

dark-haired lovers walk, arms around waists,
in el centro de the opposite
of decay

The lovers stroll in tenderness
unencumbered, shadowless
Dos pieces del sol —
hot and shining

Strangers say hello

On la alameda the end del amor
doesn't threaten with its sticky sinless arms
falsely sweet
and maimed

Lovers climb to their isla de tongues,
wrap each other tightly
in their shiny bones

Torch

I hear secret convulsive sobs from young men
at anguish with themselves
— Walt Whitman

It is late and here you are, sweaty nightmare,
old fantasy of happily ever after. Candles lit
with short wicks is what was had and where
you were headed. Furniture of hand-carved pipes,

thumping bass, white lines on glass floating
on an island of denial — props for our re-convincing.
How many hours did you spend digging yourself
in the mirror, your muscled torso priming itself

for the entry, all eyes of the temple closed tight.
Drugs pissed through veins and skin, erased,
temporarily, the truth of you — that hot raw
calling of man-love carved and re-carved

away from your core, traded for everydayness,
the ready-cut cloth. Years later the wondering of what
became of you followed by discovery: Your drive up
star-lit Tamalpais, the shower of gasoline over

your head, down your body. The match, the moans,
the month of smelling your own flesh before
getting your last wish. Your secret was the secret that stayed
hidden in the skin you couldn't live in. You could have

surrendered to Eros, unquenched angel, ghostly moth.
You could have had the god in your mouth.

LIGHT SHATTERS

so easily, leading through the odor of lovers,
through heavy-headed flowers that stare

into the dark. The full face of the moon
quavers through trees, through rotted leaves,

into a sea of silver words and ash.
When it rises on the other side of the world,

worms will have eaten its edges. A woman
will take the threads, spin a web of white

delirium to store her shards of love in,
her stunned and sleeping nightingale.

The Tyrants and the Gone Daughter

They followed sleep and hissed inside her head
Brutal ghosts who wouldn't fade into the night
They circled her like beasts around the moon
To rip out her light and leave it for dead

She felt naked clothed with many layers
And motherless though that falcon peered
Out the window to watch her walk from school
Twisting crystal beads and whispering prayers:

Please lord above bring those bullies bright love
Fill their blood with meadows and birds
Make them not too proud to cry their pain aloud
As I cradle mine, depleted mourning dove

She lived fastened to the wall, a blanched, wilting rose.
There was no shelter from those infectors
Quick black beaks shot song-less from their eyes,
Devoured her last millet of joy

In the end it was she who flew. Only her body,
Only her life. The bullies, jewel-fingered, gold
Crosses of murdered love tangled in the
Sweat of their chests, faced frozen walls, each

Alone, each nailed, each waiting on the precipice
Carved just for them, hungering for they knew
Not what in a world devoid of illumination
And love — the beginning of non-existence

Fossil

A truth that's told with bad intent
beats all the lies you can invent.
                    — *William Blake*

There was the time Erida called in Aphrodite
who was so new and light-filled with her love
and said *I know who you are and what you are*
and I'll do everything I can to get you out of here.
You'll never work again. Her job as she saw it
was to send Aphrodite running as fast as anyone
could run filled with the weight, the ten ton weight,
of self-loathing, of self-hate. No one was allowed
to speak to the young lover, no one was allowed
to listen to her either. She was placed in a palace
of fear and ignorance for eight hours each day.
One round-eyed waif of a girl whispered
I'm sorry I told her you love women; I didn't know
she'd despise you so. What is proved, saith Blake,
was once only imagined. Aphrodite buzzed her hair,
put on a tie, gnashed her teeth beneath half-closed
eyes and breathed the poisoned air all the while
doing her job perfectly perfectly perfectly each
minute of eternity. What is an office, after all,
and what is theater? She played her part thus,
until Erida, old for her years, retired to Florida
to join the other storm clouds and bitter tempests.
But as all gods and goddesses of hate do,
she held her battle tight in her gnarled hands
and one day traveled back to California to an office
where Aphrodite worked anew. Their eyes met
as she stalked through the door, a drop of spittle
glistening on her grin. *I told you*, it said,

you'd never work again. She met with Aphrodite's bossman
for, seemingly, forever and then he invited her
in. *You know each other already*, he said. *Erida, who
calls herself Ann, will consult for us, cut out the waste.* *Lovely!*
cried Aphrodite. She returned to her desk in haste thinking
the world *is* a grain of sand and watched the minutes drag
around the clock. Ann left rosy cheeked, elated in the coming
war. But it never happened, for Aphrodite told the bossman
everything and it turned out he was queer, too. *She'll never
work here*, he said. And she didn't. Once again,
thought Aphrodite, Blake had it right.
Excessive sorrow laughs. Excessive joy weeps.

MOTORCYCLE DIARY IN PROGRESSIVE MODE

My first was a 350 I learned to ride
facing a wall of baby pines on the front lawn.
She was gold with a black streak and soon
we were flying down 140 past the smell of
fried clams and frappes at Frates on the lake,
one by one the chains of existence from 17 years
back to just the day before thrown off because
this is what happens in flight and I loved
the feeling so when I left that life behind
returned home to San Francisco I bought a
400 this time maroon with a black streak
and we rode the smooth sweeping roads
down to San Diego where I felt she had been
too light for the wind traded her in for a
650 broke her in slowly to Mexico then home
to Twin Peaks and Market Street where I
lugged her slow moving hotness in the oh so
gay parade my old wedding dress dragging behind
like a forsaken cloud then up the coast and over
the Canadian Rockies where I was snowed in in Banff
gusted in in Calgary where I begged truckers to rescue us
but truck insurance doesn't cover that kind of thing
so I drove south through Idaho, past the Snake River
with its red rocks its slate shadows of hawks
down down to Sacramento where a bee caught
like a shard of glass in my scarf stung my throat,
forced me to lay that bike down in the breakdown lane
until the dizziness passed, and then we were
on to our new home in Sebastopol where I had
no garage and had to heave her up every morning
off the rush hour street like a horse knocked down
in pasture, so I sold her and didn't ride again
for over 30 years until I remembered, sweet Jesus,

time was flying by, not me, so I bought a 700,
all black, the only streak, me, a silver-haired woman
soaring solo past vineyards lagoons rivers valleys redwoods
mustard the blue meadow of sea like a bird who knows
nothing of years but everything of release and the sensation
of oneness with the thing that sets you free

Motorcycle Rispetto

When I work my tired duties
the red blood of me lies crypt cold
When I ride off on Black Beauty
I become too young to be old

Freed up to flee and hum the roads
in this moment-to-moment glee,
I twist her throttle. She explodes
past pastures to the thrashing sea.

Còmo Se Dice

— for Francisco X. Alarcòn

Once, I had a machine gun
aimed right through me.
I had been wandering the streets
of a Mazatlan barrio, camera
hanging heavy around my neck.

In doorways leading to one paradìso
or another: paper flowers, half-starved perros,
long black braids and missing teeth.

In front of el banco, a truck full of soldiers
camouflaged for the jungle stood with
rifles resting on their shoulders or
braced at their sides.
So different. So   interesante.

I raised my camera. He raised his gun.
It wasn't clear for a moment
who would shoot first. I had just come
from the coast where, for a few centavos,

a young boy opened his arms,
jumped from a cliff, flew into
the blue eye of sea. His lean body
split the surface that ate him.

North Coast Dagwood

Wind-carved trees bend to ground,
small leaves soar into air.
Over coral-colored cliffs
painted with flowers
of California light
a lone walker, north to south,
beyond the waves, beyond the world.

A gopher feeds on a berry
a woman has dropped at her feet.
What does that gopher see
with his tiny black eyes?
A sea silvered by wind,
a tossing boat,
a sky infused with fire?

Wind-carved trees bend to ground,
a gopher feeds on a berry.
Small leaves soar into air
a woman has dropped at her feet.
Over coral-colored cliffs
what does that gopher see
painted with flowers
with his tiny black eyes
of California light?
A sea silvered by wind,
a lone walker, north to south,
a tossing boat
beyond the waves, beyond the world,
a sky infused with fire?

Autumn Drift

The fog of our breath rises,
thins into a low flight
of birdless feathers.

As morning arrives, redwood
arms heavy with leaves
appear slowly against the changing sky.

Two hawks scream quick
crescendos, stream overhead.
We are together in the valley

surrounded by many, and no one.
Quails peck for seeds, jays
shriek their cranky hinges,

owls sleep with silence,
caul-draped eyes of gold marble
turned inward.

We wander down the center of the road
lined by plots of dormant color
where someone once planted their hope

for something to name.
Iris Rose Viola
Now it is day and our chill

is deep light filling

with an eclipse
of lonely mountains.

We walk and remember
keenly
fiery November stars.

Love in the Sudden Absence of

In the beginning there is something lost
and it is painful, some say   *Good.*
Wind chimes bang about over hydrangeas.
Fading blooms collect chilly tears of
(your name here). Darkness six feet under
farewell. New light waiting   just there.
A freedom not yet found beyond the bruise
of goodbye.

Yellow leaves limp-hang from the bough,
burn bright with old rain fallen. There goes
the mother, the lover, the cat, the who/whatever.
Life is Good, announces the hat, so you add
your own tag: (fill in the blank). Sometimes
loss equals extra cupcakes. Take two in the morning,
three at bed.

Sometimes it's a dog wondering *Where is she?*
as you're off licking self-inflicted wounds.
Or not. But the clock ticks over the shoulder
and the sheets eventually come off the chairs
and a body sits to remember *in the beginning*
was the ending and it hurt as it should
have hurt. Then the pain is diminished, or lost
as if she/he/it was never there. Was love?

NURSES

for CJ, in memory of Frank Decot

When you nurse a man you love
to death, feed him, pill him, drop
the drops under his tongue, when

you keep him comfortable, pain-
free, lie with him and hold him
while he cries his last earthly tears,

you become a type of mother.
When you wake one morning and find him
flown from the farewell nest

and close the one eye peeking dryly
and move his still warm fingers
to their lovely poses, you whisper

We did it, we did it. Mother,
niece, friend, wife — all of us —
which is to say the two of us:

We did it.

GYPSY MIRROR

He saw himself in his eyes —
forty different men
and as many young boys
living eighty different lives
in a dozen foreign countries.

His myriad arms and rope-veined hands
intertwined with eggs and coffins.
His tongues kissed the mouths
of the least number and the most.
They lay beached in darkness dreaming.

Tambourines and cloister bells
woke him in the mornings.
All of it was music

or sharp-tipped shovels
spooning silence

      into
           the music

THE PRIESTESS SINGS THE BLUES

after Jessye Norman, March 29, 2014

Her robe of tropical leaves
drapes softly, whispers along the floor,
along the path through ancient woodlands

to the singing spot. The long grand piano
signed by Herbie Hancock waits there
like a sacred beast, which it is.

> Falling in love with love
> is falling for make believe
> but it's also the wonder of the world
> and a rocket to the moon

The priestess sails her voice up
from the depths of darkness to the
height of glow, and every town
is lonely

Then, ivories silent, a fist pounds
rhythmically on that sacred wood

> *Another man done gone*
> *He had a long chain on*
> *Another man done gone*
> *He had a long chain on*

The fist comes down
and the high priestess sings
and the night is holy
and the moment holy

and the woman holy
and the fist holy
and the starlight holy

and now a song for Odetta
and the Blacks and Bays
and the Dapples and Grays
are holy, too

Doh wap, doh wap,
we all sing,
but the gone man,

another gone man in chains,
is still running from the dogs,
and the night is easy
and not easy
all at once
as only
a holy night
can be

Dark Syllable

> So you can believe me, in the far deeper
> sleep (these new apple leaves, maybe) we are all going
> to be perfectly all right.
>   — Franz Wright, "Apple Orchard"

Now the day is void of busy sheep
working their wool into sweaters.
Instead, they roam their green lives
sensing someone is missing that matters.

Have you flown off like a loose page or a bird
the wind has freed from our wanting palms?
You asked us to but, in honesty, we don't remember
each word of the twenty-first psalm.

But here comes your impossible pink horse
charging from north to south,
and that sober multi-eyed fly and,
so, your instruction to close our mouths.

We were all so thirsty, then remembered
we can drink forever from this cup.
You said, *The birds will keep singing
until they wake up.*

UNFURLING

Speaking as a woman under evening stars,
speaking as day draws itself up
and darkness between us comes down and raises
lightness before us, and my moon set —
as you silence my dreams from the most shallow pond
and stroke my arms as they rise in awareness,

you introduce dusk with a story never told,
ask me to meet it with an off-key sound.
O you threw your clumsy fiddle afar —
you failed at making it sing,
every note tied to your sea-green spleen
you unloosed and, yet, still clung to

And so you murmur your false composition
wondering if your words will displease
and rankle here on the high hill of sky
with its cold bent wind and a thousand paths
to home. You sing and you sing but I won't
respond though everything is felt among

blue-washed stars. Have you experienced birds
singing within compact branches, from your door
heard the barn own call? Will they encourage you
to pull your songbook out and make visible
notes for the ears of all?
Uncover your lies as well as you can.

COLD MOON

After the moon was born,
it died
and died for how many years,
how many more?
Scientists turn their backs to it
mostly —
even poets walk slowly to the sun.

The sun is life.
Its hot cushions
empty your wants
as if you had never sung dirges
or slept under a stone.

The opposite of desire
is death.
No one does a thing
to revive her.
But your foot plays foot games
to show off its usefulness.
Useful to?

Night.

A woman sails to the top of the Milky Way
stares down, her hair
longer than even love can reach.
She gets it — the rhapsodies —
here in the emerald water,
the emerald waves,
everything reaching the stars
and the stars reaching everything,
all of it finding its way

      somewhere

V
Visitations
to the Crystal Ball

Four Mirrors

Hunger

Lent is over
I can whisper things
to my body

It will finally hear me

I start a sauce
on the back burner

I cut onions
as if the thick, yellowing layers
never touch my skin

I knead dough
like a pauper who
has never known bread

I simmer a stew
while the whole universe
goes mad

and when late afternoon
finally boils over

we sit at a table
three strong women
from three generations
eating lamb and

long grain rice

cleaning plates
once empty
longing for grace

a thousand miles of earth
beneath us

Death

Yesterday we released her.
Released her dying.
Everything but her heart
lies still in us.

To the delight of her
nearest kin — the wolf —
she will be consumed
by earth. For no reason,

we never looked at her stillness,
her utter stillness, though we sang it
from our boldest stories.
Our most callous ways were mended,

clothed by a muscular kindness.
Especially the toe tips, the eyelids,
thin fragments of innocence. The question
is *Yes*. The answer is *Are they members*

of a buried treasure? We remember
she should come to us. Now. She knows
the welcoming that releases us
by her outstretched arms.

She listens as though
she has just died.
She uses our ears.
We hear her. We hear.

The Sun

rose like a dried flower
upright in the blue
throwing wide petals
of long liquid fire.

The cloud above was silent,
quiet as a dream all day,
sped its shapely body
over our eyes, turning west

toward the sea. Sun blades played
upon windows and woods,
dropped small pockets of themselves
to gutters, to ferns. In lonely times,

a raven calls out to night,
deepens blackening sky.
In the dome of our home
cool sheets of evening

rustle among cricket wings
and the redwood's perfect shadows —
those leafy arms on the screen —
capture the moans of night

perfectly.

October

Filled with dusk
withering stems become
slight brittle women.

In the movie of autumn
a full-frocked redwood
is the last shot in vertiginous green.

Darkness sings its epic
to the drop of petals
to tear up a bit until spring

paints vibrations of light
and insects birth their meals
to the birds. Infant nightfall

turns its back to the mirror
of shimmer, awakens to
a tongue of ice. In silence.

In solitude. It turns.

Visitations to the Crystal Ball

1

You sing as the newly loosed, come to the garden of dreams.
You are tinged with green, come from your traitor's proximity. Someone
watches. You know him, your jealous one.

Your jealous one discards the angels that do not brush
against him. For you, they will breathe life back deep into the root of
night, up to the canopy of rejoice.

  You want a hard splitting, something that never breaks
  in the best hour. You lose yourself to the sky. Slowly.

Slowly,
  inside the sacred wilderness,
      there is a laziness,
          a non-movement

  No one wants to desert the serenity of the snail.

The serenity of one snail mirrors many daydreamers.
Smaller than the smallest insects in the eyes of the traitor,
one dreamer says *the sea* and the sea is lit, one says
high-rise and windows burn. Without them, neighborhoods
push away from each other, push away at the tops of the hills.
They can't get far enough away

Far enough away, there is in you a cat-like settling.
You must be   very slow,   very slow
to   perhaps this,   perhaps that.

        A lifetime or two from now, you could still
        be sitting here
        blinded by the heavens.

There is a man here. A victim/izer.
The page he knew was his future
is in a forbidden book bound and lined up
against a basement wall — a blinded soldier
smoking his final cigarette.
The page doesn't satisfy him.

Beyond the page, are the children.

His greedy fingers on every off switch
make evening mean and low-down as far under the blankets
as a kid can go. He shakes the walls
with one strike of his eyes.

His heart has blistered over. Flies swarm the dead spot
of his chest; his feet shuffle its ashes
into the boards.

Beyond the boards, are the children

At night he walks the hall rubbing his hands, speaking hellfire tongues
in yellow whispers. Sheets rustle like snakes shedding young skins
in snuffed out dreams

It was the children

One of them becomes invisible, a flying girl, up to the farthest corner
where she waits for the end, observing, eternal minute after eternal minute,
waits for the end.

After he leaves the room the music begins, the singing of
one angel to another
from single bed to single bed.

It was the children

It was a long time ago and it's still in the crosshairs of night,
    bedroom doors closed against no one
        but a ghost

3

I see the blue sky sewing tightly
thin pale floats over Mauna Kea.

Not what was come for, but the real.
Here it is. Geography of a sort atop

the tallest mountain on Earth. Look below,
witness everything disembodied.

There is a calm above the impossibilities
flowing beneath your back. Red-hot tutors

of yesterday swamp every thread, every
feather, connect fragments to fragments

you thought were ash. There a door, there a
whipping belt,
love, indifference, contrition, everything propelling

their resilient ghosts into the mix of now.
White whorl of sky and cloud and water.

It's all one. An entwining bound by nothing.

4

In the past is the future

In the future is the past

Walk the garden

Read the sign:

The Time,
the little bud says,
is Now

VI
Postscript

POSTSCRIPT

The sun rises over a girl's fear
bold and intentional.

Morning's first cloud
morphs to a rose, a miracle

on a stage of blue.
The night-room lives

almost as it should,
except for the memory

of the dead-eye held steady.
Within the steady stream

and calm of light,
bird-like creatures hover horizontally,

block with feathered softness
stories of night — Day-angels.

Lo, the fear of death is nothing.
The girl is brave away from the gut

that carries threat in its jowls,
distributes it as moods require.

She lives despite it, and life is fertile.
It sings every question.

Come night, she lays down
for the first time every time.

Her blood padlocks foreboding
obscurity brings on naked feet

past the door-click. She is a moth
high in a corner. She waits

for first light. It comes.
Again and again, it comes.

What Flesh, Poetry!

A cut-away poem from *The Dharma Bums*, Jack Kerouac

What flesh, poetry!
Make a yodel-joy:
Fog, rushing ice cream,
insane nook of
mouth to huddle-cave

Sky-flower:
Get me

Notes to the Poems:

The poems in the section "Shakespeare & Stein Walk Into a Bar" use the last word of each line of the corresponding Shakespeare sonnet. Please see the foreword at the beginning of that section. An index of the first line of each sonnet appears on page 103.

"120": "Countrymen lend me" comes from Marc Antony's speech in Shakespeare's play Julius Caesar:

> Friends, Romans, countrymen, lend me your ears;
> I come to bury Caesar, not to praise him.
> The evil that men do lives after them;
> The good is oft interred with their bones;

"Còmo Se Dice"translates to "How Do You Say?"

"Dark Syllable": The poet Franz Wright died on Thursday, May 14, 2015. This poem was written in response, and in response to his poem "Auto-Lullaby"

"Dear Ashraf Fayadh": Ashraf Fayadh is a Palestinan poet and artist living in Saudi Arabia who was sentenced to death on a charge of apostasy, or renouncing Islam. Saudi authorities claim his poetry has undermined Islam and spread atheism. Due to public pressure (after "Dear Ashram Fayadh" was written), the Saudi courts reduced his sentence from death to 8 years in prison and 800 lashes. Efforts are ongoing to free him.

"Menor" translates to minor/underage. *Ay voz secreta del amor oscuro*, Oh secret voice of dark love!   ¿Poeta dulce, dónde están?, Sweet poet, where have you gone?

On May 10, 2012, the identity of Federico Garcìa Lorca's last lover was revealed. The lover, Juan Ramìrez de Lucas, handed a box of mementoes he kept of their relationship to his sister shortly before he died in 2010. At the time of their relationship, he was too young to flee to Mexico with Lorca who was in danger of assasination, and so, some believe, Lorca delayed his departure. Lorca was killed by Franco's death squads in August 1936. His remains have not been found.

"Motorcyle Rispetto": A rispetto is an old Italian form, 2 quatrains, 8- or 11-syllable lines, usually rhymed abab, ccdd, though different variations of the rhyme scheme are increasingly common, especially in the second quatrain. Rispettos may have first been written to pay respect to a woman. My motorcycle is, after all, a *she*.

"North Coast Dagwood": A dagwood is a poem whose initial stanzas are woven together to form the final stanza. As many stanzas can be used as desired. For this poem, the first two stanzas are woven together for the third. I discovered this form in Lewis Putnam Turco's *Book of Forms — A Handbook of Poetics* (University Press of New England, 2012).

FIRST LINES OF NUMBERED SONNETS:

Ave Maria, you say to me. *Hail Mary*, every moon and day	"34"	Page 26
But let us not be all darknesss and furrowed brow	"2"	Page 23
Down the hill between the roses, your suffering frame	"5"	Page 16
Heat and radiance, a hot river of gems, tend	"57"	Page 18
Hubba hubba mamacita the first line has to do with time	"12"	Page 17
If you look into the imaged skyscraper of her eye	"9"	Page 21
In number seven I tell you I have willfully ripped the light	"7"	Page 13
In the hills over Granada where my old friends the crickets	"147	Page 28
In the Torah the number 70 appears without defect	"70"	Page 19
Mama Mia, Mama Thornton, Moms Mabley	"5"	Page 15
Shakespeare & Stein walk into a bar	"4"	Page 11
She wanted to leave, to take a walk, to bend and pluck	"14"	Page 20
The newspapers are calling them the Charleston 9 now	"120"	Page 27
The white cat is invisible weaving her long	"100:	Page 22
There are spiderlings whose motherlings	"118"	Page 14
We escape our selves by walking along the shore	"60"	Page 24
What were my golden locks worth	"79"	Page 12
When love is young it rarely falls asleep	"154"	Page 25

Katherine Hastings is the author of *Nighthawks* (Spuyten Duyvil, 2014) and *Cloud Fire* (Spuyten Duyvil, 2012) as well as several chapbooks including *Slow Shadow/White Delirium* with Lee Slonimsky. She is the editor of *Digging Our Poetic Roots — Poems from Sonoma County* (WordTemple Press, 2015) and *What Redwoods Know — Poems from California State Parks*, an anthology that was sold as a fund-raiser for the California State Parks Foundation when 70 parks were faced with permanent closure. Hastings is Sonoma County poet laureate emerita, the curator of the WordTemple Poetry Series, and host of WordTemple on NPR affiliate KRCB FM. She grew up in the Cow Hollow neighborhood of San Francisco, received her MFA in Writing from Vermont College, and lives in Santa Rosa, CA. For more information go to www.wordtemple.com.